EMBRACE YOUR POWER!

EMBRACE YOUR POWER!

A *"Sistah-to-Sistah"*
Conversation

'DR. NAY'

RENEE M. WHITE, ED. D.

Published by
Hybrid Global Publishing
301 E 57th Street
4th Floor
New York, NY 10022

Manufactured in the United States of America.

White, Renee M. a.k.a. Dr. Nay
Embrace Your Power: A Sistah to Sistah Conversation
    ISBN: 978-1-951943-98-1
    eBook: 978-1-951943-99-8

Cover design by: Natasha Clawson
Copyediting by: Wendie Pecharsky
Interior design by: Suba Murugan
Author photo by: Owen Clark

Disclaimer: If you know or suspect you have a health problem, it is recommended you seek your medical or mental health professional's advice.

https://drnay.blog/

TABLE OF CONTENTS

INTRODUCTION

Embrace Your Power

Embrace your power rooted deep inside
From the world, no reason to ever hide

Your power of strength, inherent and innate
No one with the right to stifle or dictate

Your power is bold, fierce, and feminine
How you define, only you must determine

It is your woman's journey, yours alone
No one shall tell you to ever detour or postpone

You must live your life as only you desire
Not as others maliciously plot or conspire

Live in your moment, live your best life
Don't get caught up in the drama or too much strife

Nurture your own Zen and inner harmony
Accept yourself and say, "It's okay being me!"

For life is a journey, a process of transformation
As you learn from life experiences and new information

Spread your wings and evolve into the woman you are
As you shine as bright as the brightest Northern star

Follow the glowing path toward your destiny
Moving forward, you'll be amazed at all you'll see

Don't get distracted peering in the rearview
Focus on the goals that you have set for you

Always settle for only your utmost best
A thought of anything less is simply a moral test

Every achievement, be sure to celebrate
Remember, you're the epitome of what is great

So, proudly bask in your power and your glory
Manifest your most creative and joyous life story

Embrace your power!

PREFACE

"Sistah-to-Sistah" Conversations

Many women's conversations happen in the kitchen over a cup of
    coffee or tea
For us to just shoot the breeze, to vent, or desperately plea

When we assume our kitchen-table huddle
It simulates a comforting Sistah Hood cuddle

Trusting in the other's code of honor and secrecy
Appreciating the mutual support and advocacy

Girl talk is a form of meaningful discussions
Without the worry of any future repercussions

We can believe in and rely on our loyal Sistah Hood
And be assured that we'll be honestly understood

It is key for Sistahs to encourage and inspire
Or based upon the situation, even to conspire

Women share this innate bond from genetics or sheer heredity
Because our chromosomes make us creatures of much complexity

Even though we may be descendants of different families and locales
We can still form circles of Sistahs, friends, and gals

Around those kitchen tables our conversations transpire
Even when it seems like we're preaching to the choir

This book is a compilation of candid poetic conversations
With the first chapter's intent being self-love persuasions

While you're reading each poem at the kitchen table sipping tea
Perceive each one as a "Sistah-to-Sistah" conversation between you
    and me

Please feel free to engage in our vicarious interactions
And respond in the spaces provided with your thoughtful reactions

Enjoy!

INVITATION

You are cordially invited to learn more about and join the broader "Sistah-to-Sistah" Conversations through the Dr. Nay's blog at https://drnay.blog/. This website also gives access to a virtual library of Dr. Nay's poetry-reading videos.

Feel welcome to unite with the diverse Sistah community members from around the world, including regions across the United States, Canada, Dubai, India, St. Maarten, the United Kingdom, South Africa, Uganda, etc. The Sistah Hood encompasses multiple age groups and professions, including CEOs, executives, life coaches, educators, health professionals, moms, entrepreneurs, motivational speakers, clergy, etc.

For another way to view videos of Dr. Nay's recitation of poetry selections and respond on the "Sistah-to-Sistah" Conversations YouTube Channel, go to https://www.youtube.com/channel/UCmt778enj1g-0f12z6MsBRjQ/featured.

Welcome, Sistah!

ONE

EMBRACE YOUR POWER

As women, we are the epitome of strength and power despite how society may attempt to portray or perceive us. We must remember that we are the pillars of our families, foundations of our homes, and queens of our kingdoms. We are the gatekeepers of the fertile ground and we hold the master key for future generations. Therefore, Sistah, embrace your innate power! Shine as bright as the precious jewel you are!

I Am, Who I Am

I am who I am, I'm me
Not what YOU want me to be

I refuse to change or transform
To conform to meet your standard norm

Just to make your insecure ego feel better
I definitely will not be a paper doll cutter

I am not altering myself for any reason
Like a chameleon that changes colors with the season

For you, I refuse to act timid, submissive, or weak
Myself I will not modify nor tweak

Not even change a single strand of hair
Because your opinion, I really don't care

I'll never be a victim of brainwash, manipulation, or persuasion
Because I'll always be me on every attempt and occasion

I am a woman of class and, in my opinion, much sass
And if you don't like it, you can simply kiss my sweet ass

Due to my sense of self-value and self-confidence
I don't have time for any malarky or nonsense

My womanly swag is what I proudly do
Clearly, your feeling of intimidation is YOUR issue

It's unfortunate that you can't handle my powerful personality
Nor my bold and sexy sensuality

I am who I am
Never your "Bam, thank you ma'am"

Always saying, "You're too much" or "You're off the hook"
You need to seriously take another good look

I am a woman of poise, pride, and power
I'm definitely not one to take any orders, and I never cower

I am who I am, self-sufficient and self-confident
Ambitious, successful, and totally independent

To bow down and kiss the royal ring
Certainly is not my sort of thing

In conclusion, I am not the one for you
Therefore, you should seek another person to pursue

If you want me, your only option is to accept
Well, actually, it's you that I might reject

Because... I am who I am

Response:

Yes, you are who you are!! Who are you? How would you describe yourself to the world? What are your superpowers? Complete the phrase: I am who I am. I am _____, _____, _____ etc.

_____

_____

_____

_____

_____

_____

_____

_____

Believe You're a Queen

Adamantly believe that you're a queen
You have become what no mortal could have foreseen

Proudly wear your jeweled crown or tiara
And appreciate who's reflected in your mirror

Boldly take your seat on your royal throne
For there's no reason for secret flaws to be shown

Do not become preoccupied with your impurities
Because we all have some sort of insecurities

Everyone makes mistakes that we may regret
The past is the past, so never worry or fret

As a queen, perceive yourself upon a pedestal
For your divine gifts are authentically celestial

Remember that you were cultivated from fertile seed
To nourish you with what was needed to succeed

As a queen, empathetically lead throughout your destined reign
To make a lifetime of difference for all to gain

Embrace the fact that your majestic impact
Will influence with whom you have direct contact

You are a creature of a regal creed
Regarding your life, take your noble lead

Wholeheartedly believe that you're a queen
And your abundant victories will be visibly seen

Response:
Yes, you are a queen! What are your royal attributes? Describe how you want to be, and deserve to be, treated as a person of royalty.

_____

_____

_____

_____

_____

_____

_____

_____

Cherish Your Scars

Appreciate and cherish each and every scar
Because they epitomize the champion that you are

Like Social Security numbers that cannot duplicate
Your unique blemishes no one can ever replicate

They represent your life's development and growth
Some personal, others professional, or maybe both

Scars indicate your lessons and knowledge retained
And your experiences and new insights gained

They exemplify your life's challenges won
And signify the obstacles you've overcome

Some scars are physical, like stretchmarks from childbirth
While others symbolic of battles defending your self-worth

Be proud of your scratches, yet remain humble
Because you got back up when you accidently stumbled

Congratulate yourself for challenging the enemy with heed
Because it was imperative to achieve that momentary need

Your scars you should acknowledge and appreciate
Your strength and perseverance they vividly illustrate

Your life's successes are illuminated by your scars
And how you continue to strive toward the brightest stars

The strong woman that you've become, your scars you must cherish
And everyone else must also honor and indeed relish

Response:
Be proud of your scars! You are a warrior! You are a conqueror! You are fierce! Which scars have you earned as a woman? Why do you cherish them? How have your battles empowered you?

_____

_____

_____

_____

_____

_____

_____

Your Smiles

Smiles reflect positive emotions from your inner heart
Sharing happiness with your family, friends, and counterparts

Smiles can be defined as your silent laughter
That others are grateful to momentarily capture

They exemplify the sparkles and twinkles in your eyes
Opposite the dimness and gloom as you sadly cry

Smiles illuminate your eternal dazzling light
That brightens any dark room in the thick of the night

Like firework spectaculars against the midnight sky
Glistening colorful formations rocketing way up high

Or like a highly arched rainbow
With hues that vibrantly glow

Smiles can simply say, "Hey" or "Hello"
At the club when you see that cute fellow

Or smiles can convey "Yes," your utmost approval
While indirectly serving as an automatic frown removal

Like hiccups, coughs, and sneezes, there's no need to rehearse
Smiles are biological reflexes that spontaneously transpire when you
converse

Clearly, they're outward snapshots of your abounding inner joy
Setting good examples for others to voluntarily employ

In social settings, they can be quite infectious
Like viruses and yawns that are highly contagious

So, don't hesitate to smile your most vibrant smiles
For people to enjoy your companionship for a while

Smiles randomly generate their own schedule and course
Because they are channeled directly from the greater Source

Your countless blessings and divine grace
Are radiated by sanctified smiles across your face

Continue to emit your upbeat and positive energies out to the
    universe
Creating a happier world for all to experience and totally immerse

Smile! ☺

Response:

You have a beautiful and unique smile! What makes your smile special to you? What does your smile reflect from the inside out? To you, what does your smile represent?

_____

_____

_____

_____

_____

_____

_____

_____

Like Stones in a Mosaic

Women are like stones in a mosaic
Each owning its unique originality
Not needing any proof of authenticity

Women are like stones in a mosaic
Each glistening when the sun's rays are aimed just right
Brightly illuminating its inner spotlight

Women are like stones in a mosaic
Each different by texture, size, shape, and hue
Based upon the earth's pressure they've been through

Women are like stones in a mosaic
Each can withstand weather elements, rain or snow
And still be as bold and beautiful as a rainbow

Women are like stones in a mosaic
Each a product of Mother Nature
Whether stone, plant, human, or creature

Women are like stones in a mosaic
Each composed of minerals, atoms, and molecules, total
    complexity
Unquestionably inexplicable scientifically

Women are like stones in a mosaic
Each truly an object of exquisiteness
Possessing its magnificent uniqueness

Women are like stones in a mosaic
Each required a detailed intricate construction
Never a cookie-cutter mass production

Women are like stones in a mosaic
Each having a distinctive quality or characteristic
Appreciating the gift of being eclectic

Women are like stones in a mosaic
Each deserves its utmost respect
Despite the differences of any aspect

Women are like stones in a mosaic
Each as valuable as a priceless Louvre masterpiece
Worthy of a Hollywood red-carpet release

Women are like stones in a mosaic

Response:

Which precious mosaic gem are you? Ruby? Diamond? Tanzanite? What natural life pressures, and/or elements have created your unique exquisiteness? What would be your creative design to represent your personality and/or the life experiences that have sculpted you into the woman you are?

_____

_____

_____

_____

_____

_____

_____

_____

Never Dim Your Shine

Never dim your beautiful shine
Hiding under a rock or even behind

Don't step into a long, dark shadow
But allow your inner self to marvelously glow

Let your shine be of the highest gloss
And strut yourself as if you are the most powerful boss

Listen to your high heels go tat-a-tat-tat
Because you'll never be dull like a paint that's flat

You proudly exude colors that are vivid and bold
As shimmery and glistening as the metallic color gold

You're as vibrant as the robust ruby red
So, you'll never be underestimated nor under said

You'll spark global change like Shirley Chisholm
Reflecting all the colors through a crystal prism

Representing each hue of Mother Nature's rainbow
Your radiant words will resonate like Maya Angelou

Now joyously follow Michelle Obama's lead on the high road
No longer secretly traveling Tubman's Underground Railroad

You're not navigating the North Star, escaping to be free
But you're aiming to greater heights like Oprah Winfrey

Yes, you are also a woman with much to say
Because others have already paved the way

So, don't let their work and sacrifice be in vain
Let your colors shine, not being just a plain Jane

Allow your personality to luster clear and bright
That will illuminate any dark room or thick of the night

Always let your inner self sparkle and outwardly show
Never dim your shine nor your glow

Response:
What is unique about your shine? How do you plan to let it glow and brighten the world? Has anyone attempted to dull your radiance? How did you regain your glimmer? How will you utilize your power to prevent it from happening again?

_____

_____

_____

_____

_____

_____

_____

Live in Your Moment

Live each moment like it's your last
Without worrying about should or could, that's in the past

The future, no need to stress or agonize
Because your destiny is already organized

Live in your own envisioned present
No need for others to approve or consent

No one else should interfere or infiltrate
Only you should delegate and self-advocate

Nor should anyone or anything monopolize
Because you are the only one to plan and prioritize

So, live in your eternal now
And you decide your when, why, and how

Simply never sell yourself short
Because life is not a passive sport

Take a moment to stop and observe
To appreciate all that you sincerely deserve

Take time to smell the fragrant roses
And spend quality time with those closest

Do things that make you jovial and gay
Like dancing to soca or merengue

Or enjoy reading and writing poetry
Or climbing rocks, Mt. Everest, or a tree

Don't leave your bucket list undone
Be sure to have a life of hilarious fun

Your happiness is a sign of your success
Not how many people you need to impress

Live in the moment
Live in your moment

Response:
Are you living in your moment? If not, why? What do you wish to experience in your special moment tailored just for you? How do you perceive such a moment?

_____

_____

_____

_____

_____

_____

_____

Appreciate the Simple Things

You must take a minute and appreciate the simple things
And focus on fluttering your own one-of-a kind wings

You were masterfully crafted as an authentic individual
Therefore, you must live YOUR life because it's YOUR original

You should live within your specially tailored reality
And not become a wannabe reality TV celebrity

You may like to wear the latest designer fashion
Or dream of residing in a Beverly Hills mansion

Or wish to only travel first-class and five-star
Or drive the fastest and most expensive luxury car

Yes, appreciate the simple things, like food to eat
And don't worry about wearing red on the bottom of your feet

Remember that life is not about being wealthy
But what's most important is that you're healthy

So, shift your train of thought and mentality
To proudly live your wholesome life of simplicity

Appreciate that you're above and not six feet under
And enjoy the sounds of laughter's cheerful thunder

Life isn't about experiences of luxuries or enjoying amenities
But appreciating your blessings and afforded opportunities

Simply be grateful for being alive
And store your happy times in your memory archive

Response:
What simple memories are you thankful for? In retrospect, which blessings in your life are you most appreciative of that you may have taken for granted over the years?

_____

_____

_____

_____

_____

_____

_____

_____

A Woman's Strength

A woman's strength is like no other
It repeatedly surpasses any brother

Her ability to withstand painful childbirth
Demands men to respect her true value and worth

Each female possesses this mighty power
That makes every male tremble and cower

She is an extraordinary super s-hero
Who effortlessly excels to sixty from zero

She's successful as a corporate professional
While also tending to business that is personal

Her culinary skills satisfy her family's palate
As she brings home the bacon to fill her wallet

With a crying toddler bouncing on her hip
She can simultaneously perform the executive script

Facilitating a shareholders' meeting, explaining the stats
As a mother who is adorned with an array of hats

She establishes a routine and practical policy
To guarantee her administrative efficiency

A successful woman must master multitasking
To fulfill the multitude of demands that people are asking

Whether interactions with family, colleagues or friends
Mandate her to finalize and tie up any loose ends

Be assured that a woman's strength is nothing to be reckoned
For she refuses to lose or come in second

She seeks her inner strength to rule her private democracy
As a strategic attempt to create her own life's legacy

As the appointed and voted transformative leader
This woman will always rank first on any gender meter

Response:
Proudly acknowledge your strength and leadership! Share an experience when you were required to exert your power and step up to the plate to achieve a goal. What steps did you take, or could you take, to conjure up the courage to tackle the task?

_____

_____

_____

_____

_____

_____

_____

Our Life Stories

Everyone has their unique and creative life story
Daily writing a new page of their autobiography

Similar to a movie script or screenplay
The storyline unfolding day by day

As the one and only appointed scribe
The writer has autonomy to recite and describe

An individual composition of an adventurous novel
For others to leisurely read and wondrously marvel

A book comprised of chapters of various genres
With a snippet of tragedy and intriguing dramas

Revealing elements of suspense and mystique
To cause readers to sit on the edge of their seat

Everyone's original masterpiece is non-fiction
Written in a distinctive and personalized diction

Each having differed climax and plots
Serving as little windows into people's hearts

Following their life's journey and path
While enjoying their exceptional writer's craft

Therefore, as the honored listening audience
Everyone must practice understanding and patience

An adequate effort must allow for reading comprehension
To encourage undivided attention and genuine appreciation

The writer deserving of heartfelt respect for sure
Or even a standing ovation and applauding encore

Worthy of a Pulitzer, Emmy or Academy Award
The author has the right to story tell on their own accord

Everyone has their own individual life story
To share and articulate their own version of glory

Response:
What is your life story? Share a chapter of your glory with other women to encourage them to continue their journeys.

_____

_____

_____

_____

_____

_____

_____

_____

TWO

NURTURE YOUR INNER POWER

As women, we must assume a plethora of responsibilities and juggle so many hats while performing our daily balancing act. We multitask our endless to-do list but tend to put our self-care as a last priority. As a result, we get emotionally fatigued or simply "tired of being tired," feeling like a hot mess. Similar to an overheated car engine, we need time to cool off and recuperate. Sistah, you must remember to nurture your inner power! You must take care of yourself to rejuvenate your energy to help others. Therefore, routinely find time for yourself and seek your personal happy place. Enjoy some well-deserved "me time!"

∞

Self-Care

Women often assume the majority of the family's share
While last on their to-do-list is their own self-care

Because self-care is crucial for your personal psychology
Even if it's in the form of foot reflexology

Or possibly it's a hot-stone or Swedish massage
Not worrying about what the spa may charge

Sometimes you must treat yourself to happiness
Seizing quality time for your own joy and cheerfulness

Like treating yourself to a deluxe mango pedicure
Or maybe a gel, acrylic or French manicure

Or enjoying a 90-minute deep-cleanse facial
While the aesthetician makes you feel refreshed and special

Or attending a class for yoga and meditation
To slow down the pace for your sense of sedation

Whatever your choice, you must insist
That you are finally placed first on your list

Because it's key to equate self-love with self-care
So treat yourself like the MVP of the year

Remember you're worthy of the special attention
With no need to provide any explanation

So, allocate time for your routine self-care
Even if the family has to sit there and just stare!

Response:
Self-care is so important for mental health. Do you think that self-care is a priority in a woman's life? How do you self-care? How do you schedule the time for yourself? If not, how can you rearrange your calendar to accommodate it? What options of self-care might you consider?

_____

_____

_____

_____

_____

_____

_____

_____

Create a Moment of Your Reality

Take a moment and create your reality
To regain your sense of pure tranquility

Sometimes your soul you need to nourish and feed
For you to continue to flourish and succeed

Sometimes you need to make a paradigm shift
Especially when you feel like you're on the edge of a cliff

Or when you feel like you've just had enough
So fatigued and tired of being brave and tough

Seize a moment to release any stress or hostility
To rejuvenate and replenish your youthful vitality

Before you take any collateral prisoners or hostages
Plan secret escapes by creating your mental images

Imagery is essential to your mental health and state
Therefore, your spouse and kids must occasionally wait

If anyone attempts to claim that you're being selfish
Adamantly respond, "That's absolutely outlandish!"

Don't perceive yourself as a lamb for sacrifice
They must sit tight and your quiet moment must suffice

You decide which reality you want to mentally create
Because you have autonomous control of your own fate

You can imagine sitting near a crystal-clear ocean's shore
Watching colorful tropical fish swim along the blue nautical floor

Or envision yourself sitting on a rocky mountaintop
Looking out into the distance until the horizon stops

Or daydream about walking through a field of aromatic wildflowers
Admiring the arched rainbow above, crafted from summer showers

Remember, you are the sole creator of your utopian reality
Because you deserve a moment of peace and serenity

Simply, move yourself to the top of your list of priorities
And begin to enjoy the moments of your creative realities

Response:

What reality would you create just for your private moment? Where would it be? What would you be doing? Who would be there with you?

_____

_____

_____

_____

_____

_____

_____

_____

It's Okay to Say "No!"

Your option to say no is always okay
Because you're entitled to vote yay or nay

Replying no doesn't mean you're resistant
Nor saying yes as being complacent
But being true to yourself must be consistent

Don't allow anyone to persuade or sway
Your honest opinion you should always convey

It's fine to say no!
Because it doesn't define you as a friend or foe

It's not about saving face
Or even pleading your case

No one has the right to ask why, neither Dick, Jane or Moe
Simply respond with, "Because I said so!"
No need to evolve into a battle like the Alamo

You have the right to your opinion and personal space
Therefore, sometimes others need to be put back into their place

Often women try to satisfy everyone else
Now consider making decisions to delight yourself

Simply wanting some quiet "me time"
Is not a misdemeanor or a felony crime

Cure your "I can't say no" disease
And focus on you as the one to please

What you want, you must self-advocate
And be sure with others to communicate

You must establish your perimeters and your boundaries
To eliminate any future questions or unwelcomed inquiries

This dialogue doesn't have to be difficult or controversial
Just keep the conversation focused and cordial

Practice in the mirror and the words will flow with more ease
And the nervousness and anxiety will eventually begin to cease

Always remember, no one has the authority over you
Clearly, reclaiming your own power is way overdue

It's okay to say no!

Response:

Do you have difficulty saying no? What are some phrases that you can say next time to prepare you with a declining response to someone's request? Remember, you have the right to say no.

_____

_____

_____

_____

_____

_____

_____

A Slippery Slope

Sometimes life can feel like a slippery slope
When you feel like you can no longer cope

So many things written on your to-do list
That you feel like you desperately need a psychiatrist

Feeling like a hamster running 'round a spinning wheel
As you only want to just stop, surrender, and take a kneel

Wanting to stay hidden under the blankets in bed
Wrapped snuggly from your feet to your head

Feeling like you're standing on a cliff's peak edge
About to fall from a skyscraper's window ledge

Yes, life can sometimes feel like a slippery slope
But you must learn to pace yourself and adequately cope

Learning how to slowly count backward from ten
And knowing to say enough is enough exactly when

Understanding when to positively self-talk
Or when you need to take a long, scenic nature walk

Taking deep breaths and just slowly breathe
Knowing that you'll survive and truly believe

Understanding that everything is relative and temporary
So, no need for you to constantly fret and worry

Honestly accepting your raw emotions and how you feel
For you to effectively and mentally heal

Yes, life can be like a rollercoaster, with dips and dives
So, we must determine how we want to live our lives

Do we want to live a life feeling uptight and stressed?
Or live a life feeling happy and blessed?

But one thing for sure, we must always embrace hope
Because life can sometimes feel like a slippery slope

Response:
What is it in your life that feels so slippery? What factors are slipping out of place? What do you think you need to do to get some traction and control of the situation? Take time to self-reflect? Meditate? Seek spiritual guidance? Talk with family or friends? Seek mental health assistance? Always remember that the wheels will eventually stop spinning and you will steadily resume along your highway of life. It's okay to ask for help.

Facing My Fears

I won't let my life be led by fear
Taking my reins and decisively steer

Like a monster under a child's bed
I will not let scary words circle in my head

Like a kid afraid of a dark room
I won't let fear linger nor periodically loom

Like a kindergartener's first day of school
I will perceive fear as miniscule

As tightly as the child hugs his teddy bear
My confidence will secure my struggle with fear

Neither will I be afraid of that empty closet
And allow the unknown to unjustifiably inhibit

I will not give any power to fear
Openly and boldly I will bravely stare

Directly in fear's terrifying face
Not permitting it into my personal space

The scary monster of fear I will gladly behead
Because my life won't allow to be negatively led

Yes, I will no longer embody fear
Or allow obstacles to easily scare

Like a baby's unstable first step
New challenges won't make me appear inept

Even with a stumble or a fall
My decision to get back up will be my call

I will steadily strut with pride
Beaming success from the inside

I won't exude evidence of any fear
Rather embrace what I truly care

Proudly, I will do the jig and happy dance
Now knowing that fear hadn't the slightest chance

I will continue to laugh in the face of fear
Because no longer will I allow negativity to adhere

Response:

What fears do you have? Are you allowing them to block your dreams? Provide an example. What are some strategies that you can implement to face your fears?

_____

_____

_____

_____

_____

_____

_____

_____

I'm a Hot Mess

I feel like I'm a hot mess
As I'm dealing with so much stress

My head is jammed with a bunch of jumble
Feeling like it's about to just burst or crumble

My brain neurons sparking every which way and everywhere
As if the wheels are churning fast, but I'm still going nowhere

Rapid thoughts and ideas flying in every direction
That I can't maintain razor focus nor any mental concentration

Right now I'm a mental and physical mess
I could use a fashion designer to even help me dress

I know that my hair is the cause for the sideway stares
But really, at the moment, I really don't notice or care

I know that I need to pull myself back together real tight
As I get my mindset and attitude back just right

I cannot wallow in sorrow and self-defeat
But stand tall and strong on my own two feet

I must not stay consumed in any distress
Nor continue to label myself as a hot mess

I realize that I must not do you but do me
I've learned that is the solution and master key

My worries and problems I should start to focus on less
To uplift me out of this episode of hot messiness

I will only target the many things that I did good
I won't concentrate on my would, should, or could

When I start thinking positive and not on my mess
That will be a definite signal that I've made some progress

Response:
Have you ever experienced an episode when you felt like a hot mess?
What was going on in your life at that time to put you in that slump?
What steps did you take to pull yourself back together? Do you have
any strategies now to prevent you from reaching that low point again?

_____

_____

_____

_____

_____

_____

_____

_____

Not Feeling Yourself

Lately, your life seems so routine and mundane
Thinking you're losing your mind and going insane

It feels like your true self is trapped deep inside
And your inner spirit wants to privately sneak and hide

You go through the same daily motions day by day
As your happy emotions seem to sadly rot and decay

Early in the morning when you get out of bed
It feels like you're not awake but like the walking dead

Feeling as if your soul is bewildered and roaming lost
Like you're completely disconnected from life and your Source

Feeling so drastically isolated and totally alone
That you don't even want to be bothered talking on the telephone

You feel as if your soul only wants to hibernate
But you know that you need so desperately to rejuvenate

You're just so tired of feeling so doggone gloomy and sad
That sometimes you try to brush it off as just a phase or a fad

But you intuitively know that something psychological isn't quite
    right
Assured that you'll eventually counter it and put up a good fight

Be careful to not quickly make judgments and label as depression
Always obtain a medical diagnosis from a therapist of the profession

Never worry if you'll be stigmatized or people will foolishly
    criticize
Because we'll always perceive you as a brave warrior within our
    eyes

We have all experienced some unhealthy mental state
Something that we can all honestly and personally relate

Therefore, you must reach out to your friends and others
And accept the helping hands of your sisters and brothers

Don't further ponder the idea or continue to contemplate
Shamelessly take the leap of faith and no longer hesitate

So, seek the love and assistance without further heed
To fill the empty void of love that you emotionally need

Escape those solemn feelings that you so desire to dismiss
By encircling yourself with caring friends, embracing their affection-
    ate kiss

Be assured that there will be a happier tomorrow and after
As your rejoiced spirit bursts with smiles and joyful laughter

Response:

Are there days when you just don't feel yourself? When you are not at that state of equilibrium, what is your quick fix to lift your spirits? What is your guilty pleasure? What puts a smile on your face on those gloomy days?

_____

_____

_____

_____

_____

_____

_____

It's a Temporary State

Remember it's only a temporary state
So, don't allow it to become your altered fate

Your current thinking and mentality
Definitely will frame your future reality

What you concentrate on in your mind
Will be what you, in real life, will actually find

Don't waddle in your saddened sorrow
Because the hardships will continue to follow

You simply can't perceive your issue as permanent
It'll only solidify in your life, like masonry cement

Because what you envision, you can magically create
Therefore, you can imagine your problems to dissipate

What you truly believe and actively think
Can instantly appear as quickly as an eye blink

Never believe that the situation is simply bad luck
Because it's not where you want to be eternally stuck

You must not easily succumb to defeat
But view your life as wholesome and complete

So, don't become preoccupied with your current trouble
Focus on your blessings that will be bestowed in double

Hold fast to your avid faith and belief
And your problems will eventually grant some relief

Don't become deflated and discouraged
Instead, conjure up your bravest courage

Be sure to never say never
Because your issues won't last forever

Sometimes, you must pull back and patiently wait
And you're given the green light to your true fate

This temporary state may have an extended time frame
But hold tight to the belief that it's not your end game!

Response:

Remember that the road of life has curves and potholes, but eventually the path will straighten and become smooth once again. What are the current bumps in your roads? How are you handling the rough terrain? How do you foresee your future travels?

_____

_____

_____

_____

_____

_____

_____

_____

Tired of Being Tired

I'm so tired of being tired
For a job that I was somehow anonymously hired

The position requires me awake at the crack of dawn
To fulfill the secret oath that I have privately sworn

My job responsibilities mandate me to wear a myriad of hats
There are so many, that I can't even ramble off the stats

I'm the cook, the chauffeur, and the babysitter
I'm even the one to clean up their mess and dirty litter

I make everyone else content and happy
But I must adamantly ask, "What about me?"

I'm so tired of being tired
And my family hasn't a clue of what's required

I'm the expert and jack of all trades
Magically turning everyone's lemons into lemonade

Behind the scenes everyone I must organize
Without them even realizing nor even recognize

I covertly keep them all on track
And I don't even get a thank you or a pat on the back

I clean the house and daily cook
But my needs how do they always overlook?

I'm so tired of being tired
At times I want to be self-fired

It seems as if I'm always on the go
While they look at me sideways if I begin to slow

It seems like a never-ending juggling act
To keep the home and my career intact

Keeping everything and everybody up to par
Have I neglected myself and gone too far?

I'm so tired of being tired
Now I contemplate becoming self-retired

I'm the first awake in morning and last to bed at night
As I've continually tried to keep up with all my might

Over the years, I've passed every test by doing my very best
Now it's time to give myself an overdue and well-deserved rest

I've decided to no longer meet everyone else's expectation
But take some "me time" and go on a relaxing vacation

I'm so tired of being tired

Response:

Are you feeling tired? What are you tired of? Which hats are you currently wearing? How can you better balance your juggling act? Do you need to take off some of your hats? Do you need to realign your purpose? Do you need to get better organized? Or do you simply need to rest and regroup? Utilize this opportunity to assess your emotional needs.

_____

_____

_____

_____

_____

_____

_____

_____

Seek Your Happy Place

Take the time to seek your own happy place
Where you can secure that safe, soulful space

A place where you can have inner peace
And where you can totally self-release

Where you can align your chakras with the Universe
And only with yourself fully immerse

Not concerned about others to pacify
But focused on your own spirit to gratify

Simply seek that location where you can quietly sit
Because you should definitely believe that you deserve it

Yes, confidently find your own happy place
Where you can briefly quit life's rat race

A place where you can simply be alone
Even if it's in the bathroom, sitting on your golden throne

Or consider walking among nature's beauty
Where healing your inner soul is your rightful duty

Yes, find that special place where you can just sit
And listen to nothing but the peaceful quiet

A place where you can reach a grounded state
And take a moment to reflect and meditate

A time when you can remain emotionally still
To appreciate the feeling of being serene and tranquil

A moment where there's no one else to appease
And everything outside of you comes to a halting cease

Yes, seek your own personal happy place
And find the time to slow down your hectic daily pace

Remember that it is imperative to tend to your spirit
Even if you must mend it snippet by snippet

Response:

What is your happy place? How do you obtain that inner peace?
Do you dedicate a special time to nurture self? How can you work
toward this important personal goal? What steps do you take?

_____

_____

_____

_____

_____

_____

_____

THREE

CHANNEL YOUR FEMININE POWER

As women, we all share a unique genetic chromosomal attribute and possess a special Sistah Hood bond. Even though we may live in different regions of the globe, we have universal experiences and emotions as female beings. We travel our unique, yet parallel journeys of life through womanhood despite our locale. Therefore Sistah, whichever phase of life you're in, motherhood or menopause, you must channel your feminine power and embrace the true woman that you are!

Our Woman's Journey

It's amazing how just yesterday we were little girls
With fairy tales in our heads dancing and spinning in twirls

During the teenage years we seek to discover our individuality
While exploring our self-defined identity and sexuality

As young ladies we have plenty of fun as we maintain our reputation
And still be responsible building our future's foundation

We begin our careers and contribute to our retirement
Being devastated about how much money goes to the government

Some of us decide the option of partnership or marriage
And sometimes before or after comes the baby carriage

We assume a myriad of roles as professional, spouse, and mom
Juggling these many hats with only one arm

We are so busy keeping up that the years and decades fly by
Unbelievably, as quick as a blink of an eye

When we reach the fifty-year-old mid-life crisis
We finally realize that time doesn't have any biases

We try to turn back the clock and rekindle our youth
At the same time attempting to accept the truth

We will finally be able to retire and collect our pension
Enjoying our golden years traveling and cruising across the ocean

Our grandkids running behind us in quick pursuit
While we are deciding what to pack, the red dress or pant suit?

Our woman's journey is a timeline of our development
And a mirror of our legacy and our life's accomplishment

Be proud of your journey!!

Response:
Which aspect of your journey are you most proud of as a woman?
Where do you perceive yourself along your journey of life? How do
you want to further develop and mature as a woman? Have you met
your personal expectations thus far?

_____

_____

_____

_____

_____

_____

_____

The Truth About Age

Age is not just about a numerical digit
But your time and what you did with it

It's about your positive energy and longevity
Your zest for life, thrive, and vitality

Despite your age, you stay young at heart
Inside, remaining that child you were from the very start

Through the years, you continually grow and refine
As your inner self radiates and brightly shines

At a young age of twenty-three
You were anxious for all there was to see

But even at a mature thirty-five
You still felt excited and much alive

Now, being a vibrant and sexy fifty-six
Don't worry about what to repair or physically fix

Like contemplate any snip and tuck
Or a little here and there lipo-suck

Don't dreadfully count the passing years
But laugh and enjoy the happy tears

Interact and cherish family and friends
Attempting to see things from their perceptual lens

Celebrating and cheerleading each other
Valuing and respecting each as a sister or brother

Simply live life to the max and utmost
Like travelling the world from coast to coast

Not randomly checking boxes on a bucket list
But trying new things that you cannot resist

Never say that you're getting so old
But become more daring, fierce, and bold

Live a fulfilling life and nourish your soul
Don't let life's challenges take a devastating toll

With new opportunities, you open each new door
Be willing to question, seek, and explore

Life is about evolving through developmental stages
Better understanding as you turn the multiple pages

Each chapter you'll have a different point of view
Because each time you are a different version of you

Again, age is not only about counting a number or digit
But the evolution and refinement of your everlasting spirit

Response:

How do you define age? Do you think that it should dictate how a woman should act, dress, or achieve? How do you feel about your age? Should/could you feel differently?

_____

_____

_____

_____

_____

_____

_____

_____

Girlfriends

Girlfriends are your loyal and devoted allies
Who will expeditiously serve as your private eyes

They will do for you whatever they can
Like a trustworthy, right-hand man

True girlfriends are there through thick or thin
They'll come to your rescue whenever you say when

They will peep through windows like a secret agent or CIA spy
If you have any unanswered questions about your partner or guy

They will hold your hair back in the bathroom stall
When you've consumed way too much alcohol

They will offer their gentle shoulder for you to cry
When your unworthy significant other abruptly says goodbye

Girlfriends share their good times and bad
Some are like sisters that you've never had

They will sit up with you all night eating ice cream
While you share each other's fascinating dream

They will dance and party with you at the club all night
Then drive home giggling until the early-morning sunlight

They will go to the mall and walk store to store
Until their legs and feet cannot step anymore

Girlfriends are your priceless and invaluable assets
That could never be discounted at any of the best outlets

They'll even testify in court and plead for mercy
To defend your innocence during any legal emergency

You know that they are just one call away
To share your exciting news or your dismay

Their love, encouragement, and support are a must
Because they are someone in whom you place your highest trust

Response:
How might you define a "good" girlfriend? Has your definition changed with age and/or life experience? What are the most important characteristics and why? Share examples of some behaviors demonstrated by good girlfriends.

_____

_____

_____

_____

_____

_____

_____

_____

Sistahs From the Block

We are all Sistahs from our hometown block
Amazing how fast hands spin on the face of a clock

We are upstanding ladies from around the way
And I am a proud member, I must definitely say

Now we're all successful women of our special Sistah Hood
While once we were little girls from the same neighborhood

We played every day up and down our friendly street
Running around on our sneakered and jelly-shoed feet

Traveling back and forth to each other's home and yard
Not having any concerns of fear to take into regard

We were truly a close-knit community
Where we built the foundation of our lasting sorority

Our loving parents cared for us all the same
As we played our thrilling childhood games

We raced our bikes speeding down the street
Trying to peddle the fastest, the winner to beat

We chased down the singing ice cream truck
Then later, having flying dodgeballs to quickly duck

With the guys we also played spin the bottle and kickball
Sometimes scratching our knees when we would fall

In the garage, we played Truth or Dare
Having to kiss a boy, we really didn't care

We played hopscotch and jumped Double-Dutch rope
But one thing for sure, we never smoked any dope

Nor did we affiliate with any street gangs
As we wore our pigtails, afros, and bangs

Innocently, we had clean and wholesome fun
As kids blasting those water-filled guns

Yes, we enjoyed the block parties and barbeques
Eating and dancing, up and down our 134th Avenue

Oh, those good, old times are such happy memories
Because we were, and still are, extended families

Response:

Who were your childhood Sistahs? What were your favorite childhood games or activities? Share a "happy" childhood Sistah memory. Are these women your girlfriends now? Why or why not?

_____

_____

_____

_____

_____

_____

_____

_____

Motherhood

As a woman, you're welcomed into motherhood
Not knowing exactly what to do, or even should

Motherhood comes with no instructor's manual nor book
So now you have a new responsibility and different outlook

Usually it's a process of "learn as you go"
Or what other mothers have told you so

You try to problem-solve and figure it out
Without a meltdown or a frantic shout

Especially when the baby cries all night
You do your best to stop it with all your might

You change the diaper or give the pacifier
But things still seem to remain so dire

You continue to try to figure out what to do
As you're the one who starts to turn blue

You hope that it's only colic or gas
That will eventually start to pass

Thank goodness, the baby finally starts to quiet down
Because now you can't tolerate another sound

The baby begins to sleep and peacefully rest
With you knowing that you did your motherly best

You slowly learn the tricks of the trade
As your worries and anxiety of motherhood begin to fade

You learn that you need a regular bedtime
And adding cereal to the bottle is not a crime

You know the perfect temperature to keep the milk warm
And how to hold your sweet baby snugly in your arms

As you gently glide in that rocking chair
Your child won't detect any distress or fear

The key is to be confident and stay calm
So, the baby won't sense any hurt nor harm

Simply, babies need to feel safe and secure
And you can do those motherly duties for sure

As a mom, you learn that kids need only your love and care
That you are so willingly ready and able to share

Response:

As a new mother, are/were you confident in this demanding role? Does/did it feel overwhelming? How might/did family and friends support you? Never be too proud to seek assistance if needed.

_____

_____

_____

_____

_____

_____

_____

_____

As a Mom

As a mom, it's your duty to cultivate and nurture
Providing your children with a routine and adequate structure

Whether you're a mom of a girl or boy
Their birth rings your heart's bell of pure joy

You're elated by the baby's ten toes and little wiggles
And totally thrilled when they say, "Ma-Ma" and giggles

You teach your kids the alphabet, colors, and math
Sometimes having to chase them down the hall to give them a bath

As a mom, you want to protect them from any pain or hurt
Automatically willing to offer off your back your only shirt

You may reminisce about when they were in the terrible two's and
    three's
But in retrospect, those energetic toddler years were a breeze

When they're teenagers, you may have to visit the principal at school
Advocating for them because they got into trouble trying to act cool

You may give unsolicited advice and worthy guidance
Instead, they perceive you as being overprotective or a nuisance

A mom must strike a balance of leniency, to ensure not to enable
While creating an environment that is wholesome and stable

As children grow up and begin to branch out into the world to play
As a mom, you hope that you've taught them how to stay safe, and
pray

When your children become adults and have kids of their own
They'll finally understand parenthood and the responsibilities of
being grown

Take pride that you've done your job as mom well
How they raise your grandkids, time will definitely tell

Response:
If you are a mother/grandmother/auntie, what do/did you enjoy most
in that role? If not, what did you appreciate most about your mother/
grandmother/guardian as a child? If you plan to be a mother in the
future, what do you anticipate or look forward to most in this mater-
nal role?

_____

_____

_____

_____

_____

_____

_____

The Woman's Body

The woman's body is a natural wonder of intricate design
Perfectly and creatively tailored as a one of a kind

Each patented with distinctive features that are extremely precise
Like those voluptuous hips and perky boobs to sometimes entice

As a young girl, no one mentions anything about menopause
Or a list of other possible undesired issues or flaws

Like the menstrual cycle that's secretly referred to in code
Until one day, a girl sees red while sitting on the commode

But every female learns to appreciate these characteristics
And doesn't concern herself with the gender statistics

Obviously, each female's body is totally different and unique
Not deserving of any evaluation, criticism, or critique

Some are perfectly shaped like an hourglass
As they strut their strut with plenty of sass

While others replicate the curvature outline of pears
As they confidently walk and provoke those manly stares

Clearly, women come in a multitude of shapes and sizes
But it's what inside that's important, as everyone realizes

Therefore, at every age, she must focus on her health
Because it is of the greatest value and acquired wealth

She must monitor her daily intake of calories and glycemic grams
And endure required annual pap smears and mammograms

Later in life she must test her bone mass density
Because strong bones are a dancing girl's necessity

A woman must ignore those old wives' tales and myths
Instead, follow her own physical body and mental shifts

Despite her level of maturity or which developmental stage
A real woman is phenomenal and extraordinary at any age

Response:
Always love every inch and curve of your physical being! What do you appreciate most about your body? What is the greatest attribute that you always like to accentuate? Why?

_____

_____

_____

_____

_____

_____

_____

Orgasm

Every woman deserves a toe-curling orgasm
To feel her vaginal muscles quiver and spasm

Ladies, don't be ashamed of a little masturbation
Every woman needs an exhilarating sexual sensation

It promotes a healthy physical and mental state
A self-remedy when you're up at night late

Many women easily lie to their man in bed
With fake compliments swelling his ego and his head

As a woman, you hate to kiss and tell
But sometimes you must ask a girlfriend, "What the hell?!"

Unfortunately, a grown man may pre-ejaculate like a young boy
That's when you masterfully pull out your exotic pleasure toy

Whip that sucker out, that's snugly in your nightstand
And you can be the lead drummer of your own one-man band

The buzzing mechanism always takes you to the tippy top
And only you are the one to decide when it should eventually stop

Conveniently, you can adjust the speed, from slow to fast
And you also decide how long for the orgasm to delightfully last

Faithfully, it always perfectly hits that G-spot
As you determine how many times, a little or a lot

Yes, Mr. Rabbit is always steady and readily available
Just nickname your vibrator, Mr. Cum Incredible

So, when you're lying there all alone
Remember how to calm your frisky hormone

He's there waiting when you're awake and lonely
Mr. Rabbit is your "go-to guy," the one and only

Despite the color, the length or the girth
The financial investment, it's definitely worth

Your handy-dandy gadget is guaranteed to energize
Don't be even slightly inhibited to willingly utilize

It strategically causes your body to convulse and explode
Then decide if you want another or end your orgasmic episode

When you're finally satisfied and had enough
Leisurely, sip a glass of wine or take a cigarette puff

Final note:
Always keep a standby AA battery
Or a steady source of pure electricity! ☺

Response:

An orgasm is a healthy bodily function. Have you ever experienced an orgasm with a partner? Have you explored your body privately to achieve orgasm? Have you considered a sexual toy? Do you feel that you are sexually inhibited or shy? Why? Do you desire to have more sexual freedom? What steps might you take to feel more comfortable?

_____

_____

_____

_____

_____

_____

_____

_____

Menopause

As a young girl, no one talks about menopause
She only hears is that human nature is the cause

The details and symptoms are left untold
Until she learns more as she turns 50 years old

She now knows that estrogen takes a halt and pause
A hidden menopausal stipulation and contractual clause

She experiences those intolerable steamy hot flashes
And the stunted growth of eyebrows and eyelashes

She battles the plague of itchy, dry skin
Splattering baby oil for that youthful glow again

The mid-life period, not at all pathetic
Because she's still alive and energetic

No woman should be considered old or weak
Because in actuality, she is at her life's peak

No longer worrying about responsibilities of childcare
She has raised her kids and has had her nurturing share

A menopaused woman is liberated
Who should be applauded and celebrated

She has acquired a newfound level of freedom
And has definitely accumulated a wealth of life's wisdom

Her motherly duties begin to cease
So now she can do whatever she please

Instead of fulfilling those family obligations
She can travel on her dream luxury vacations

A mature woman can still dance at the club all night
Gyrating her hips with all her womanly might

Because the sex drive doesn't at all diminish
As the lubricant suppositories moisturize and replenish

The mornings after, she can now sleep late
Telling her grown kids that they must patiently wait

Yes, menopause should be perceived as a life's celebration
And not conveyed with a negative connotation

Menopause should not be portrayed as cynical
But positively described as a mature woman's pinnacle

A rewarding period of life for total transformation
With fulfilling opportunities for her wholistic rejuvenation

Menopause is not a curse or taboo
It's a time when you're finally the best version of you!

Response:

Do you believe that 50 is the new 30? Is there a correlation between biological and chronological age? Did/has anyone spoken to you about menopause prior to that phase of life? If you are menopausal, how do you perceive it? Is it the best time of your life or not? Why?

_____

_____

_____

_____

_____

_____

_____

_____

Retirement

It's never too early to plan retirement
To enjoy the golden years in any event

Elders may be older and more mature
But all deserving of a fabulous time for sure

For years they've raised their kids and worked hard
So now, their responsibilities and worries they can discard

Therefore, despite your age, plan to retire
And compose a bucket list that you can aspire

Elicit creative ideas from your mind and heart
Ranging from river rafting to eating a la carte

You can dream of a 21-day Mediterranean cruise
Where you can relax in your cabin and freely snooze

Or if you desire some adventure, like skydiving
You can also consider jet skiing and racecar driving

Or if you want to visit Paris, the Maldives or Dubai
You can consider first-class Emirates to luxuriously fly

Whichever decision for your dream vacation
Definitely will be an absolute thrilling sensation

So, whatever excites you or floats your boat
You will totally enjoy yourself and proudly gloat

Immediately begin contributions to your retirement pension
To alleviate any future financial vacation tension

Whether you monthly deposit a dollar or a dime
The account will accrue interest over time

No need to worry about the amount of social security
Because you will secure your economic stability

You will financially advance beyond your peers
To experience a joyful retirement during your golden years

Simply remember that you only live once not twice
So, it's your life that only you to decide if it will suffice

Response:

Have you retired? Is it what you expected? If not, how do you perceive your retirement years? When do you anticipate retiring? What do you plan to do? Are you saving and preparing for it? What steps do you need to take toward your golden years' goal?

_____

_____

_____

_____

_____

_____

_____

_____

FOUR

BASK IN YOUR POWER

As women, we are often conditioned to be caregivers and more concerned about others' needs than our own. We tend to postpone our dreams for that "right time," such as the children graduating school or after the husband gets a promotion. But what about your dreams? How do you envision your destiny? Just believe, if there is a will, there is a way. Yes Sistah, you can live your best life! You can move forward, even if taking baby steps. Always be confident to bask in your power! Enjoy your journey of real transformation!

∞

Always Walk With Confidence

Always walk your walk with confidence
Because you're walking with your ancestral inheritance

Your family heritage is your private traveling cohort
Who will always offer their loving spiritual support

For generations they have nurtured your family's homestead
To guide you along your life's path ahead

Be assured that you're not walking alone
For the footprints to travel have already been shown

Ancestors' past struggles have stabilized your pillars
Serving as present time role models and exemplars

So always walk with an upward tilted chin
Because you're uplifted by your guardian angels and eternal kin

Always walk with your head held high
Do not appear at all timid or shy

Always walk with your spine vertical and straight
Claiming your birthright to emancipate

Always walk with that confident, sultry strut
Even feel free to swish that feminine butt

You are a woman of power and grace
Yet as delicate as fine Burano lace

You are a woman who believes in her significance
Who values her life's true existence

You are a woman, beautiful and proud
Who demands attention in any large crowd

You are a woman who exerts an exemplary first impression
Who confidently displays her unique self-expression

Therefore, always walk with confidence!

Response:
Yes, always walk with confidence. What are you most proud of as a woman? List your 3A's: Assets, Achievements, and Aspirations!

_____

_____

_____

_____

_____

_____

_____

Focus on Your Vision

Always focus on your vision
What it is, is only your decision

You must imagine and define in your mind
Then what you mentally seek, you will realistically find

Don't get distracted by unnecessary confusion
Or any falsified misconception or illusion

You must clearly visualize where you want to go
So that you can properly plan for it to happen just so

You must decide how you want to smoothly transition
Because your life's objective is your personal mission

You'll be amazed at your powerful and influential impact
Even if the person may not immediately say or instantly react

So, continue to proudly work toward your vision and plan
Making the world a better place, no matter where you walk or stand

As a teacher and mom, you willingly inform and educate
Not knowing the other issues that you effectively eradicate

At times, you seem to do what you're instinctually told
As positivity and goodness miraculously unfold

You should be proud and amazed at the positive differences you make
Thoughtfully taking others' lives and hearts at stake

Embrace and acknowledge the success of your goal
So, never ever let yourself be undersold

Never minimize all the good that you do
Because others really do appreciate and love you

Always believe you're making a world of difference, and that's a fact
So, please give yourself a pat on the back and a bit more slack

Remember, you are an intricate piece to the puzzle and masterplan
Your significance to the world you may not yet fully conceptualize
    nor understand

Therefore, expeditiously pursue your vision and goal
Because you truly have a heart worth more than 24-carat gold

Response:

Stay focused! Keep your eyes on the prize. What is your ultimate vision? No goal happens overnight, so what steps do you need to take to reach your aspiration? List your plan below. Remember... be patient and stay diligent!

_____

_____

_____

_____

_____

_____

_____

Live Your Best Life

Life should not be just a matter of survival
But a life of your soul's renewal and revival

Live your life of exuberance with substance
A life of many blessings and abundance

Believe that you're worthy of life's luxury
Believe that you're special and extraordinary

Enjoy the finest wines recommended by the connoisseur
Or the uniformed chauffeur opening the limousine's door

Charter a private jet to the islands of the Caribbean
Or cruise on a luxury yacht across the Atlantic Ocean

Relax after a hot stone massage at a five-star spa
Or sip on a champagne sangria at a Tapas bar

Sail on a riverboat down the Nile
Or hike up Kilimanjaro in single file

Listen to the Philharmonic at the Met
Or at Lincoln Center watch a ballet duet

Eat a chef-prepared breakfast with bloody Mary's
While planning fun-packed daily itineraries

Whatever you decide is your preference
Use your Likert-scale as your reference

Life should not be just work and chores
But opportunities to explore the world's distant shores

So, don't let costs discourage or sway
Because if there is a will, there's a way

Begin to save your spare nickels and dimes
And look forward to future memories and happy times

Grab onto life like the horns of a bucking bull
Enjoy your ride of adventure and live to the full!

Response:
Are you living your best life? What do you imagine as your best life?
Create a vision with descriptive detail, vivid color, and true passion.

_____

_____

_____

_____

_____

_____

_____

Always Move Forward

You must always move forward to achieve your goals
Not peering backward while fulfilling your soul

Oftentimes you want to travel fast like an L.A. freeway
But moving slow is okay because you're still on the right pathway

Even taking tiny baby steps is still progression
So, don't become impatient and initiate any regression

Never succumb to your current circumstances
Think how efforts will increase your greatest chances

You must resist the negative feeling of discouragement
Instead, stay positive and rev up your level of encouragement

It is advisable to stay optimistic and enthusiastic
Understanding its counterproductive to be pessimistic

Never claim that your goal is too complicated or far-fetched
You must devise a blueprint that is well-detailed and sketched

Develop a comprehensive plan with smaller increments
And later implement any necessary changes or supplements

So, keep your keen eye on the predestined prize
And continue to reach farther and steadily rise

Remain reassured and stay on course
Because if you don't try, you'll experience remorse

You would never know what is possible
Or of what you are incredibly capable

Even if you feel outside the comfort zone or awkward
Take a deep breath, a footstep, and always move forward

Response:
Where are you strutting in those stilettos?? How do you feel as you travel forward? Embrace the emotions and the absorb the positive vibes. You must wholeheartedly believe in your efforts and walk forward with true faith.

_____

_____

_____

_____

_____

_____

_____

Fling Open Your Door

Fling open your door
To achieve your true destiny and so much more

Seek your purpose and ultimate goal
To spark the fire within your internal soul

Fling open your door
To stretch and spread your wings to freely soar

Don't just crack the door and bashfully peek
But swing it wide, step out, and bravely seek

Fling open your door
Not being afraid to cross the threshold and further explore

Don't let bold ideas intimidate
But use them as tools to motivate

Fling open your door
To determine what your bright future has in store

Don't perceive your door as closed or shut
With thoughts of excuses or even the word "but"

Fling open your door
And be confident of your own wisdom and acquired lore

Steadily turn the doorknob and swing it wide
To courageously prosper while searching outside

Fling open your door
To attentively listen to your instinctual gut and inner core

Reflect from inside and you'll miraculously uncover
Aspects of yourself that you will amazingly discover

Fling open your door!

Response:
Do you partake in self-reflection? Do you question your thoughts and actions to better learn about yourself? Don't be afraid to open that door and discover what is behind it. But remember, you are always organically evolving and growing with time.

_____

_____

_____

_____

_____

_____

_____

It's None of Their Business

It's none of their damn business
Your life doesn't require an outside spectator or witness

Your decisions are only yours
You don't need anyone to voluntarily judge your flaws

You shouldn't care what others have to say
Only if you've told them they may

People seem to think they can offer unsolicited advice
So, tell them, "No thank you" once or even twice

No need to be abrupt or rude
Just be quick, direct, and shrewd
Simply tell them nicely, "Do not intrude"

Eventually they'll learn to mind their business
If they don't want to suffer the consequence

You have the right to your own privacy
Not needing someone else to help you determine your own legacy

Graciously tell them, "It's none of your business"
And send them off disappointed, with a hug and a kiss
Appreciating their love and concern, as your big bro or sis

Response:

Do family members/friends tend to meddle in your business? Explain. How can you politely tell them to give you your privacy? List some prepared phrases for the next time someone offers unsolicited advice.

_____

_____

_____

_____

_____

_____

_____

_____

Think Before You Act

Always think before you act
Because your reputation you can negatively impact

Don't blindly jump in to take the lead
It's useful to first observe and sometimes take heed

Before you talk, speak or even shout
Take time to learn what the venue is all about

You need to sit and listen like in school
So that you don't end up looking like a fool

You must consider how yourself you want to portray
And what you want to appropriately say

You must adhere to the parameters and what they expect
Without acting in disregard or causing any disrespect

Determine how you can fit in and complement
Without causing any hard feelings or any resentment

Success requires you to be a team player
Not running around acting like a naysayer

For others to really appreciate your talent and gift
Sometimes you must make a paradigm shift

You must modify your approach for whatever the show
For your uniqueness to truly shine and readily glow

It's okay that your boldness and confidence you want to convey
But you must strategically plan to do so in a positive way

You must always think before you act
That's for certain and that's a fact

Response:

Have you ever regretted a situation where you presented yourself in a negative manner? Explain. If you could turn back the clock, how would you have changed the scenario? Because you learned from the past, how would you prevent it from occurring again?

_____

_____

_____

_____

_____

_____

_____

_____

Just Stand Still

Sometimes you need to just stand still
And let your spirit's vessel fill

You must embrace your moment of silence
To accept your divine guidance

Not hearing a whisper nor a sound
Only the rhythm of your bleeding heart's pound

Letting your inner gut tell you where to go
Whether it's travelling fast or taking it slow

You must listen to your voice within
To lead to where you're going, not where you've been

Simply, follow the path to your destiny
As you navigate your personal journey

Just stand still and innately feel
And take your hands off the steering wheel

Release your grip from the gears and not steer
Instead, be faithfully led without any fear

No need for a GPS, globe, or a map of the road
Because your navigation will be instinctually told

Sometimes, you need to just stand still and not hear
And your self-direction will be crystal clear

Just stand still and wholesomely believe
And trustingly you will know when to stay or when to leave

Response:

Are you a constant planner or do you take a moment of silence to allow things to naturally unfold? When have you stood still and something manifested? Share. Remember that sometimes you can tirelessly churn your wheels deep into the mud and go nowhere. But what is truly meant for you, will always be there waiting for you.

_____

_____

_____

_____

_____

_____

_____

_____

The Rearview Mirror

Stop peering through the rearview mirror
Because looking through the windshield is so much clearer

When you look toward the rear behind
You know exactly what you will find

Looking from that backward view
You will only relive what you have been through

You must bravely look up ahead
And see where you will surprisingly be led

Excitedly anticipate all there is to see
Especially all of the unexpected opportunity

Always make sure that your windshield is crystal clean
So that you can see exactly what there is to be seen

Faithfully continue to drive toward the unknown
And the correct roads and streets will be eventually shown

You will travel on the right highway and freeway
As you're guided in your unique directional way

Directed to the perfect exits and right turns
Where you can explore and further learn

Gliding smoothly up and down the hills and bends
Sometimes against the strong westward winds

Aligning with the path's twists and curves
Not being afraid, but having the adventurous nerves

If needed, widely open your car window
To stay alert to where you must forwardly go

Clearly, it's difficult navigating in reverse
Therefore, your future you must embrace and immerse

So always keep your eyes on the road up ahead
Not looking behind in the rearview mirror instead

Response:

The question is: Where are you headed, not where are you coming from. What destination do you want to see in your windshield? What direction do you have plotted on your roadmap of life? Take your time driving at the speed limit, watch out for bumps in the road, and take any detours if necessary. Your destination will be there patiently waiting for you.

_____

_____

_____

_____

_____

_____

_____

Transformation

As women, our perceptions change at different ages
As we continue to develop like a butterfly's life stages

During certain phases of women's lives
We consider ways to revive and revitalize

We seek to experience rejuvenation and transformation
Like a butterfly's miraculous rebirth and reconfiguration

As a butterfly departs its cocoon in early spring
Its brilliantly colored wings begin fluttering

We also want to spread our beautiful wings to further fly
Compared to the life cycle of a monarch butterfly

We aspire to become even more stellar
Like the transformation of a butterfly from a caterpillar

Because sometimes we want to make a little change
Or something that we intend to purposely rearrange

Similar to a butterfly changing in its chrysalis
You can also go through your own metamorphosis
But you must decide where to place emphasis

Determine which qualities you choose to accept or reject
So that you can successfully reinvent or self-resurrect

Whatever it is, it must be of your own desire and will
Maybe it's to continue your education or learn a new skill

Maybe you aim to live a healthier lifestyle
Or you just wish to rest for a while

Or maybe alter your perspectives and outlooks
By reading more self-help books

Whether you adjust an aspect that is physical
Or modify an issue that is mental

Only you decide how you want to self-define
So that your goals and actions will congruently align

Like a butterfly perched on a flower's petal
You determine where you want to settle

Even if you decide to, or not, make any alteration
Be assured that you will still be a fabulous sensation
Because remember, you are a unique, one-of-a-kind creation

Response:

As a maturing woman, have you witnessed your transformation over the years? What changes have you experienced? Were they due to specific life incidents or situations? Are there any aspects of growth that you would like to further develop? Why? How do you think you can utilize your power to initiate such self-development?

_____

_____

_____

_____

_____

_____

_____

_____

EPILOGUE

Thank you, My Sistah

Thank you for sharing a part of you that is sacred
The secrets, the truths, and the naked

Each poem was based upon my personal experiences
And my actual, true, real-life instances

I'm optimistic that you've enjoyed my stories told
And you value my womanly advice like a pot of gold

As you read my book, I hope that we were able to connect
And you've decided I'm a friend that you would gladly select

Our honest dialogue has been a real blast
Therefore, I hope that our vicarious friendship will forever last

Friends must share a bond and camaraderie
To just relax and feel free to be who we want to be

So, love who you are and love who you want
You shouldn't feel that you need to put up a phony front

Always remember that you are a gem and a jewel
And be careful manifesting your selection pool

Always move forward to achieve your ultimate goal
And seek opportunities to enrich your soul

Remember to do what is beneficial for you
Don't worry about what others have to say or do

Stay true to yourself and your written responses
Always keep an open heart and maintain a clear conscious

When you feel the need to pick up your pen
Don't hesitate to reach out to me to talk with a friend

Thank you again, my Sistah, my newfound friend!

DEDICATION

First and foremost, I must thank my beloved mother and dear Sistah ancestors who genetically created and nurtured me into the woman I am today. As a little Black girl from Jamaica, Queens, NY, they instilled in me the importance of pride, strength, and respect. They taught me that with self-confidence and diligence, I could achieve any goal that I set my heart on. These incredible female role models groomed me to Embrace My Power! I adamantly believe that the pages of this book reflect the many lessons learned from these powerful women wonders!

I must acknowledge my sisters and Sistahs who have encouraged and supported me during my journey, including times of triumphs and tribulations. I appreciate my Sistah Hood that represents a genuine circle of reciprocal uplift and empowerment. Thank you, Sistahs!

ABOUT THE AUTHOR

Dr. Renee M. White was affectionately nicknamed "Dr. Nay" by family and friends when she earned her doctoral degree of educational leadership at the University of Virginia in 1995. She is currently a full professor, teaching literacy and cultural diversity. Dr. Nay initiated her career over thirty years ago as a NYC public school elementary teacher upon graduating New York University. As a native New Yorker and former NYC public school student, she now teaches higher education and resides on Long Island.

From the perspective of a mature woman and divorced mother with two adult sons, Dr. Nay writes motivational poetry for a diverse audience of women. She shares a variety of insights about women's experiences regarding life and love. Through her poetic craft, Dr. Nay promotes women's unity, encouragement, and empowerment.

Readers are invited to continue the "Sistah-to-Sistah" Conversations through her blog at https://drnay.blog/ and/or her YouTube Channel at https://www.youtube.com/channel/UCmt778enj1g0f12z6Ms-BRjQ/featured.

In addition, she facilitates Sistah Pod workshops encompassing a myriad of interesting topics, where Sistahs share their expertise and knowledge with one another.